"A fun and informative read. Entrepreneurship is not an easy path for anyone, and the twists of the journey can easily be glossed over. Michelle Mazzara has given a real insight into the personal and professional challenges that were part of building Luvafoodie®. I appreciated the journey from dating website to candy maker to spices. Truly a story of a brand that knows how to pivot. I can hardly wait to try a couple of the recipes!"

—Julie Finch
Trademark, Copyright, Social Media and E-Commerce Attorney, Finch Law Office

♥

"Michelle Mazara's story is about a woman whose resilience is a joy to behold. She brings us along on her journey of pain and success. We read about her being knocked down and wonder how she always found a way to bounce right back up again. When one way of succeeding was blocked, she persevered until she found another way to achieve her dream. A must-read for all who share Michelle's dream of making themselves better but encounter a world saying they are foolish for trying."

—Stephen Nowicki, PhD, ABPP
Charles Howard Candler Professor of Psychology Emeritus, Emory University and Author of
Choice or Chance: Understanding Your Locus of Control and Why It Matters

"Michelle Mazzara has displayed courage and perseverance in her journey while building the Luvafoodie® brand by facing numerous challenges head-on. Her determination to overcome obstacles inspires those around her. Through her actions, she has become a true testament to the power of courage and unwavering resolve."

—Jeanette Tostenson
Qwiznibet Foods Co-Owner

♥

The Making of Luvafoodie® Brand is an inspiring narrative about Michelle Mazzara's ability to turn her dreams into reality against numerous obstacles. Whether you're a food lover, an aspiring entrepreneur, or simply looking for motivation, this book is a must-read. It serves as a reminder that with passion and perseverance, anything is possible. As someone who is in the same industry, I read the entire book in one day and could not wait to turn the page. "

—Dean Packingham
Founder, Mike and Jen's Hot Cocoa

THE MAKING OF

Luvafoodie®

BRAND

How One Woman Launched a
Clean-Eating Revolution

MICHELLE MAZZARA

Luvafoodie® CEO and Founder
Luvafoodie.com

Library of Congress Cataloging-in-Publication Data

Mazzara, Michelle
The Making of Luvafoodie® Brand: How One Woman
Launched a Clean-Eating Revolution

p. cm.
Paperback ISBN: 978-1-947708-30-3
Ebook ISBN: 978-1-947708-44-0
Library of Congress Control Number: 2024920712
First Edition, October 2024

CITRINE
PUBLISHING

State College, Pennsylvania, USA
(828) 585-7030 · www.CitrinePublishing.com

For information about special discounts for group purchases, please call
(828) 585-7030 or email Info@CitrinePublishing.com.

For Mom, Lucy and Daisy

and

For the Lovers and Foodies

♥

To Your Health!

CONTENTS

In the Spotlight

Strange Times

CONTENTS (CONTINUED)

INTRODUCTION

At Luvafoodie, our mission is to help people eat clean and stay well. We believe in using simple, natural ingredients to create delicious, healthy meals that are packed with flavor and nutrition. Our spice blends make it easy to add flavor and nutrition to any dish, without relying on unhealthy processed ingredients. Our tagline is *Eat Clean, Drink Clean, Be Well and Stay Well.*

This book is dedicated to all those entrepreneurs who have found the courage to follow their dreams. Being an entrepreneur is not for the weak or faint of heart; it takes a strong mind and body. I always knew one day I would start my own successful brand and company; I just didn't know what the brand or daily life would look like once the idea found me, or how many learning experiences there would be on the way to success.

It is my hope this book will be inspirational for others who are traveling to find their purpose and destiny. It is with courage and hope that you will arrive at a place in life that will make you happy. Happiness is internal; it is something we create for ourselves, versus relying on others to make us happy. I learned this from an early age. I figured out I had to make myself happy first. I guarantee the uphill battle will be worth the pain and struggle. Many people will quit along the way. Life has no instruction or manual to live by. It is a series of mistakes, trials, wins, losses, and happiness—all of which help you arrive at your desired goals and destiny.

My life journey has taken several paths, without any boundaries. I have found it to be a combination of successes, struggles mixed with pain, and happiness.

This book highlights the ten years of building Luvafoodie® brand from scratch into a consumable brand. In 2024, the company turned ten years old. At this point, I felt ready to publish my story.

I hope it motivates whoever reads it to find their inner voice and heart before it is too late. Life is short; the sooner you figure out what your purpose is and who you are, the happier you will be. I found myself at forty-nine, so it was later in life that I found inner peace and happiness.

Defining moments are significant, life-altering events that happen at different ages. Defining moments are often painful and significant instances or periods in our lives. We never forget those defining moments because they leave scars from the pain. As time goes by, the painful, defining moments become part of us and we live with and learn from them.

If our defining moments are happy or joyful, we will also never forget those moments because they left us with joyous memories to look back on and smile. The choice I have made is to accept the defining moments, the painful and the joyous ones. My defining moments shaped me to become a strong, independent, ambitious, loving woman. I found faith and a spirit in myself during the journey. I found I could love unconditionally and that I deserve to be loved as much as I love. Now I won't settle for a mediocre life or love that does not feed my heart and soul.

I hope you enjoy reading my journey that launched with a dream and led to building a brand that feeds people body and soul, starting with my own.

♥

PRE-LUVAFOODIE®

Luvafoodie®

1970s

I knew I had an entrepreneurial drive early on. As a little girl, I bought several colors and types of ribbons and made them into barrettes. I convinced my mom I could sell them in stores and to friends. It was a challenge for me at only seven years old to sell as many barrettes as I could, and I loved it.

♥

In college, I created a company called Bella Baskets. I bought wholesale bath products and other goods from the Minneapolis Mart and used them to make and sell themed gift baskets. I also created a company called Celebration Make-Up. I would provide makeup services for brides. Neither company was a much of a sales success, but each company taught me how to manage bookkeeping and fulfilled my entrepreneur drive.

♥

1980s AND '90s

After college, I started working in sales for a large New York City costume jewelry company. I was able to stay in Minnesota as a territory representative for the company, one of the largest costume jewelry companies in the 1980s. It was my first job that provided a company car, selling and merchandising to small department stores. I had the largest personal collection of necklaces, earrings, and bracelets anyone could ever want.

After three years, one of the largest cosmetic companies in New York City became my new employer. I was again fortunate to stay in Minnesota as a territory manager. I worked my way up in the company and was promoted to district manager and then to regional manager. This experience was invaluable to my career. I learned to sell and negotiate and manage people. The '80s were a different time—there were no boundaries in management.

I climbed the corporate ladder to my desired position as a national account manager by the time I was thirty, selling to Target Headquarters. Over the course of my years in sales, my main two accounts became Target and Walmart, the two largest retailers in the country. My sales career allowed me to travel for work and pleasure. I earned a nice salary that allowed me to purchase a nice home, travel, and any other things I wanted or desired.

Beyond supporting myself financially, I learned to be tough and develop a strong mental business sense. I was in sales for National Accounts, so that made me feel like I was in a fishbowl. Selling and managing for two of the most important accounts, I had all eyes on me from corporate and management at every company I worked for. I learned to play with "the big boys" and develop a thick skin. In a couple companies, I was the only female salesperson in the management group. I witnessed many verbal and nonverbal gestures that would have gotten my peers or bosses fired had I said anything. The business environment in the '80s was very different to what it is today. There was no Me Too movement, and men dominated in sales and upper management at most of the companies I worked for.

However I chose to look the other way and keep playing on their playground. In hindsight, I should not have turned the other cheek, endured, and looked away. But I was too afraid to lose my job or get fired. I knew one day if I owned my own company, I would not tolerate any of the remarks and comments I endured.

♥

In a nutshell, I have always had big dreams and been very ambitious in achieving most of the goals I set for myself and my career. I had wanted to be a National Account Manager and sell to Target Headquarters since college. I became a National Account Manager, selling to Target when I was thirty. I achieved this goal, and I was proud of it.

♥

SPRING 2000

At thirty-five years old, I created a company called Vino Arte. The story behind this company was based on love. I was dating an Italian man who lived in Venice. I had applied for a finance visa and needed to have a job for him once he moved to the USA. Thus, I started to make glass-ornament wine charms to hang on the stems of wine glasses. I traveled to Sicily, Italy, by myself and tried to sell them in Italian stores. This was a unique and somewhat scary experience for me. I was by myself, speaking little Italian, walking into stores in Palermo, Italy. It was an experience, and I will leave it at that! You may wonder what happened to the Italian man and Vino Arte. They both ended. However, my Italian ex-boyfriend is still a friend of mine and because of him, I know how to make delicious risotto and bolognese sauce.

♥

SPRING 2010

In my mid-forties, the large food-consumable company I was working for decided to close all business units in the USA. The brand continued to exist but under different names. All business units were sold off to other companies. I was out of a job at forty-five and faced with what I wanted to do with my career.

I was burned-out of corporate America, and I knew in my heart I would one day want to start my own business and sell my own brand. I was good at sales and knew I could sell anything. I was often told by people, "You're a good salesperson, and *you sold me!*"

I did some contract and freelance work for a couple of years, working in the pet industry for two startup companies that are no longer in business. I have always loved pets and liked learning about the pet industry. I became familiar with the pet industry while traveling to national pet trade shows.

FALL 2013

In addition to doing contract work for pet companies, I had started cooking and creating recipes. I was a natural at coming up with different recipe combinations and creations. I had spice jars and different flavors of olive oils and vinegars in my kitchen. I started to enter a lot of recipe contests. I was winning many small ones, but then the big one came along. I entered the Eighth Annual Cavit Wine Pizza Contest. I started making pizza recipes at home out of my kitchen. I entered a pizza recipe that consisted of roasted garlic, eggplant, caramelized onions, and mozzarella cheese. I ended up winning the grand prize, which was a trip for two to Italy. The trip included a tour of the headquarters of Cavit Wine in Trento, Italy, their vineyard in the province of Trentino, Italy, as well as a few days in Venice. I went with one of my girlfriends and had an amazing time. I stayed on for a few extra days and went to Florence, Italy. I took some cooking classes and learned *a lot.*

Once I arrived home, I went on several TV stations, sharing my award-winning pizza recipe. This is when I had the idea to create a brand called Dolce Vita USA and to create my first cookbook. In Italian, "dolce" means sweet and "vita" means life. Thus, the idea of the Dolce Vita USA brand was to represent the "sweet life" in America. I created a website under the name Dolce Vita that featured my recipes. I became a regular cooking segment contributor on My Fox Morning News on the Buzz Hour in Minneapolis. This was the beginning of my becoming a local TV cooking personality in the Twin Cities of Minneapolis.

♥

BEGINNING YEARS

Luvafoodie®

SPRING 2014

One month before turning forty-nine, I went to see my friend and psychic, as I had occasionally done over the years. I met Kathleen at a party when I was thirty-five, where she did my first reading. Her attention to details about my boss and job at the time were spot on, and this was the beginning of our friendship. For this reading, I asked her what she saw in my career future. She said, "You will start your own company. All your previous work for corporate America has prepared you to start your own company."

I had the skill set and mindset to start my own company. I just had to figure out what that company was going to *be*.

The psychic was not very specific. She said I would have a website and it would be managed by others. I would sell things and often be seen on TV doing cooking segments.

Memorial Day Weekend, the same day I saw the psychic, I woke up at 4 a.m., which is typical for me. My best ideas come to me between 3 and 4 a.m. Good thing I was told to always keep a notepad by my bed so I could write down my ideas. Lying in bed, I said to myself, *I should start an online dating website for foodies.*

There is no dating website out there geared for foodies. What would I call it?…I know…I'll call it "Luvafoodie."

BINGO! A light went off in my head and that is how Luvafoodie® was born.

The next day, all the missing pieces came together and I knew I needed to start an online dating website for single foodies. The only problem—I knew nothing about creating a dating website, WordPress, or where to begin. Tenacious by nature, I now had a goal and a unique idea. The next step was to get an IT team in place to build the website with content I wanted to create. The questionnaire people would fill out to enroll in the dating site needed to relate to food and beverages, and we needed to figure out how to match two people together using their answers.

Typically, I would have set a timeline for the website to be completed. It was a huge goal to bridge an idea that started the first of June to going live on August 19. It was an even bigger goal to decide I would launch it on Fox TV. I was fortunate enough to have a relationship with a producer, since I had been cooking on Fox TV doing cooking segments for my brand Dolce Vita USA for the past year. The producer scheduled me in advance to air this new dating foodie website. My team and I worked every day, and my deadline to go live on August 19 was accomplished. When the website launched, it was not a hundred percent perfect and there were glitches that needed to be fixed.

We faced many challenges in the first six months. The biggest was how to monetize the website. I needed critical mass to be able to charge members. After attending an international online dating conference, I quickly realized that I was in way over my head. There were three companies that made up the online dating website world—three companies that spent millions advertising and attracting singles to their platforms. Then there was the other 5 percent of us that were niches and would seemingly never be able to attract the same critical mass as the big three.

My concept was great in theory, but I did not have millions to spend on marketing to get critical mass in every city. Thus after about seven months of launching Luvafoodie, I started to have serious doubts. I was doubting myself and wondering how I was going to make a living.

I am a highly creative person by nature, as well as a great salesperson. I knew I had a great name and idea but maybe needed to expand the brand into consumables. The vision statement for Luvafoodie® was to connect people who share a passion for food and beverage. Having something to consume with the brand name Luvafoodie® made sense and tied into the website.

The first consumables I created were all-natural, homemade artisan caramels. I knew a good confectioner who could make them fresh for Luvafoodie. There were three flavors: sea salt, raspberry, and bacon. They were delicious and creamy, and customers loved them.

I only planned to sell the caramels online under our shop tab. However, a couple months after launching the caramels online, around when Luvafoodie® turned one years old, I was able to get them into specialty shops and grocery stores. Then I was facing weekend demos, living in a grocery store Thursday through Sunday. It was a vicious cycle because the caramels did not have any preservatives in them, so the shelf life was short. I kept track of which stores had my products that would expire soon and would go to the store and hopefully sell them all so that store didn't lose money. I was too small to give any store credits for expired products. I also had to fund all the caramel samples. I had gotten myself into a no-win situation. I started not to feel good in September and began to feel a lot of stress at the demos. I would come home from the demos tired with chest pains and became convinced I had a disease.

♥

SUMMER 2015

Turning fifty was a defining, growth-packed year for me and Luvafoodie. I started to realize that in order to make Luvafoodie® a consumable brand, I needed to transition to more shelf-stable products. The more products I could sell, the more money I would make. I started to think about what other food categories could expand the Luvafoodie® brand.

I made the decision to launch several items in new categories for Luvafoodie. The spice blend subcategory was small, and I knew if I came out with some delicious blends, it could make cooking and grilling easier for the average home cook. The grilling category was big, and there was seasonality I could capitalize on. I created four original spice blend flavors: Garlic Lovers, Jamaican, Honey Mustard, and Steak. I would later reformulate them and come up with several new blends. The creation of each new blend is what I enjoyed most about launching a new flavor.

♥

DEFINING MOMENTS

Luvafoodie®

2016

One word describes 2016—*ouch!* It was the year that changed me and defined who I am and what I wanted for the rest of my life. It was the year that I changed my thought process and outlook on life with a completely different perspective. It was the year I found out I was going to have a once-in-a-lifetime experience. It was a year that I continued to expand and be innovative with new items. It was a year that I would never, ever have been able to predict or foresee. I could only look ahead and move forward. It was the most intense year of my life, emotionally and physically. It was the year I became spiritual and started to pray for God to be in my life.

It was the year that I decided I needed to write this book to inspire others, the year that I started my journey in helping others. It was the beginning of me knowing I was not supposed to just create Luvafoodie® as a brand, but I was going to build a brand with a story and a purpose. It was the year it all started to make sense—what I was supposed to do with my life. It was the year I could say all my past experiences, good and bad, prepared me for what I went through.

What I learned is that courage is facing your fears one day at a time. Fear is bigger in your head than in reality. The inner voice knows a lot more than you want to admit, and believe me, *trust it.*

I learned my will to fix things, to make things better, is what drives me every day. I learned at the end of the day, it is not about what I did but who I impacted. I learned that I am a strong woman with a will and determination within me stronger than I knew.

I learned that I could survive on very little sleep for several days in a row before my body and mind said, *Time out.* I learned that everything I had accomplished was because I worked 24/7 and never gave up. I learned that I am not a quitter and quitting, to me, symbolizes failure. I learned the most important thing—that I wanted to give my love unconditionally. That is what I wanted more than anything else. I learned to love in a way I never experienced or felt before. I learned that this was the reason I had to start my company, so I would reach this higher level of feeling.

♥

SPRING 2016

I decided to launch my new grilling spice blends at the Minneapolis Food and Wine Show in March of 2016. The spices were a big success, and I started selling them into grocery stores in the Twin Cities. I was able to secure distribution of the four spices in the meat departments of Kowalski's markets and Hy-Vee Grocery stores, which were new to the Minneapolis area. Customers loved the spice blends, since they were easy to use, preservative-free, and all natural. I saw this turning into a spice business. The idea was simple—to create healthy blends of spices and herbs to use easily on meat, chicken, and seafood. Spice blends allow the customer to use just one mixed blend versus purchasing several separate spices to use on meat and seafood. Luvafoodie® spices were different from many of the spice blends in the marketplace because they had no anti-caking agents or fillers, whereas most of the large spice companies add a lot of fillers to their blends. In addition, the first ingredients are often sugar, salt, and silicon dioxide (an anticaking clumping agent).

The spice category is a hard space to be in because there is so much competition. Also, most grocery stores already have their own private-label spices. There are also low margins in the spice category. That said, I was fortunate to have a group of local grocery stores in Minneapolis add my four spices to their meat departments, which also involved me doing weekend demonstrations in their stores.

Lowes Foods in North and South Carolina also added Luvafoodie® spices to their Smokehouse stores. Thus, I was successful, had distribution in a competitive retail space, and was getting sales. I started to do cooking segments on local TV shows. This allowed me to increase my sales and build awareness at a local level in states beyond my home base.

In addition to launching spice blends, I decided to launch a few drink mixes. I created an all-natural mulling spice mix, used to make mulled cider or wine, and a new winter Hot Toddy mix that could be served hot during the holiday season and winter months.

Still, I was not feeling well. I told my family in May 2016, "Something is wrong with me. I have a weight on my chest and pain that never goes away."

I thought to myself, *Do I have lung cancer? I've never smoked a day in my life.*

My Mother said to me, "Well, you don't have cancer, and if it were your heart, you would be dead by now."

My brother said to me, "It's your company—the stress of selling and your financial stress. That's all it is."

My intuition told me regardless of what they were saying to me, it was getting worse, and the pain never went away.

I thought I had a variation of a mock disease called Demoitis. Every time I did a demo, my chest pain was worse and I could barely stand the pain. I'd endured this pain for almost a year now. I had seen my doctor in September and complained about chest pains and shortness of breath. My internist told me I had costochondritis. He said, "Don't worry. It will go away on its own."

That was the beginning of me being misdiagnosed. I had a family history of heart disease on my dad's side of the family and my cholesterol was high. My doctor should have ordered an angiogram at that time.

♥

This was a defining day for my company Luvafoodie. Over twelve months, I had been in contact with the Business Connect Team who was managing the 52nd Super Bowl, to be held in Minneapolis, Minnesota, in February of 2018. It was my goal and desire to become a vendor and be part of this once-in-a-lifetime event. I developed a line of chocolates and Hot Chocolate on a Stick with the Super Bowl in mind. I knew I needed to have samples of products to give to the committee at the time of a potential meeting.

I was invited March 31 to pitch my brand "Luvafoodie" to the Super Bowl committee. It was an honor to be one of the few companies selected to have this opportunity. I first had to meet the committee's requirements, which were to be a minority-certified company in business for at least three years and to be a Minnesota-based company. The Super Bowl was looking for the best in a class of three hundred companies. The companies selected would be published in the NFL Resource Guidebook in June 2017. They would have the opportunity to work with contract companies to provide their services or products for the ten days of events leading up to the Super Bowl and during the big Super Bowl game.

I knew my pitch and product offering had to be the *best* I could do. I had the NFL Super Bowl logo made on chocolate bars and cookies. I put together a football-shaped basket filled with cookies, chocolates, and Hot Chocolate on a Stick as my product offering. I dressed for success, wearing the colors of the logo. I had three minutes from start to finish. I rehearsed and rehearsed my pitch and timed it out perfectly. It was a huge success, and the panel of judges loved it. I could tell by their smiles, acknowledgement, and compliments at the end. It truly was a happy, defining moment. I nailed it and I knew it! I had to wait to find out officially if Luvafoodie® was selected, but I felt confident.

♥

SUMMER 2016

I turned fifty-one July 2. I was busy with my products and weekend demos on spices and candy. Most weeks, I did demos from Thursday to Sunday. I had sold the spice blends into stores on the premise I would do store demos. Thus, I had obligations that kept me in stores every weekend, and I had been doing demos, either on candy or spices, for a year and a half. I had no social life. Occasionally I'd go to Happy Hour or have dinner with my mom. It was a grueling schedule, and I was tired of selling every day.

My physical was coming up at the end of July. I planned to tell my doctor that I didn't think I had costochondritis.

"Doctor, I still have chest pains. In fact, they've gotten worse and my cough and shortness of breath are worse. I am afraid to go sleep at night because I don't know if I will wake up. I honestly think I am going to die."

My doctor said, "Okay, well, since your cholesterol is 330 and you're not overweight and you exercise all the time, maybe we should have you get an angiogram with contrast, just to be on the safe side."

I thought, *What?* I agreed to schedule the diagnostic angiogram at the hospital, but due to a nurses' strike, I was not able to get in until August 29. It was hard to believe someone with chest pains and a family history of heart disease needed to wait one month to get a test scheduled at a hospital.

During those thirty days of waiting, self-doubt started talking to me. *I should cancel the angiogram; I really don't have time. I think this is a waste of time. I am too young. I am sure it is just stress, but I can barely walk a mile now, so what is going on with my body?*

I convinced myself I should cancel the angiogram and told my mom the week before I planned to do so. Fortunately, she said, "I think you should keep the appointment, since your doctor ordered it. Then you can stop complaining about your chest pains because you will know it is nothing but stress."

I agreed. "Okay, I will keep the appointment."

♥

When the day of my angiogram with contrast arrived, I was feeling this was a waste of my time. I was young, and everyone else in the waiting area was old. I was sitting there thinking, *I wish I had canceled the appointment.* The nurses were on strike, so I was even more upset about being at this hospital.

I have very small veins and they had already tried twice to get the IV in me with no luck. After the third attempt, they called for the IV team to use an ultrasound to find a vein that would work. I got in the gown and went into the scan room. I was feeling very stupid. I thought, *The nurses must think, This woman should not be here.* The nurse technician walked me through the x-rays and when to breathe and exhale. I had to take a nitro at one point to get an important x-ray. The test was over, and my mom was driving me home and said, "Now that everything is okay, you can put this out of your mind."

Two days later, I was on a conference call that morning before going to a new store for a meeting. My cell phone rang, and I missed the call. It was my doctor's office calling. I called back and got their voicemail. After about three calls back and forth, the nurse left me the message that I needed to call back and ask for my doctor's assistant and they would connect me. I thought, *Why not just leave me a voice message that everything is okay? This is more time wasted out of my busy day.*

I made another call and asked for the assistant. This time, a nurse got on the phone. She told me the results were back and I had 80–90 percent blockage in my right anterior descending artery. My doctor wanted me to make an appointment with a cardiologist immediately. I was listening and thinking, *This is surreal. I can't believe what I am hearing. Who is she talking to— not me?* I really couldn't believe this information.

I was in complete shock. I got off the phone and called my mom. "I just got a call from my doctor. I have 80–90 percent blockage in my right anterior descending artery."

My mom was in disbelief. She said nothing and we sat in silence on the phone. I started to cry—not a lot, just a little—because for some reason, it didn't really sink in.

Next step, I called to make an appointment with a cardiologist. He couldn't see me until the end of September. I took the appointment. Three hours later, my doctor called me back and said, "Michelle, you can't wait until the end of September. We don't know what percentage of blood is getting into your heart. You need to call back and say you need to get in this week."

I agreed and arranged a meeting with the cardiologist for the first of September. The next couple of days, I continued to live my life like nothing was wrong. I didn't tell anyone other than my mom. I felt ashamed— maybe not a typical feeling, but that is what I felt. I slowly realized I needed to tell the rest of my family and a few close friends. I have always been a private person and not one to share a lot on social media, so I chose not to post on any social site. This was my personal problem, and I did not want the public to know about it.

♥

FALL 2016

The day before my procedural angiogram, a surgery to have a stent put in, I was at a winery picking grapes. The winery was a customer of mine, and I had promised the manager I would do a social media post of the grape-picking event. My chest pains were unbearable that day, and halfway through the grape picking, I had to stop and sit down.

That night, I thought I was going to die and not make it to the hospital. I decided to try not to sleep but stay awake, so if I had an attack, I would at least know it. I had spent the past two and a half weeks living my life, working, and going about my business. I had updated my will that summer, so I knew everything was set if something should happen to me. My company, Luvafoodie, would shut down because I *am* Luvafoodie. I had no partners or investors. I had a contract team who managed my website and vendors who made products for me. I was not worried, and I was not crying.

The day of my angiogram at the heart hospital in Minneapolis, I was strangely not nervous. I took pictures outside the hospital in front of a statue and recorded a video that I later deleted. I would say a big part of how I felt included denial.

I was, on the other hand, upset that the nurses were on strike at the hospital, and I was fearful my care would not be good. My fear was substantiated by the next twenty-four hours. The angiogram was not running on schedule. I was in a gown and ready to go into the cath lab. My IV felt uncomfortable, and I was wondering if it was put in correctly. I had requested the IV team to put it in, but after they could not find the team for two hours, I agreed to a nurse doing it. This was my mistake as a patient. *Trust your instinct.* Again I had those small, troublesome veins that required a couple pokes before they could get an IV in correctly.

It was time to go to the operating room. I shed one teardrop as I said goodbye to my mom and brother. The cath lab was sterile and had huge bright lights and rock music playing. It felt like what I'd seen on TV shows when they go into an operating room. I was moved onto a hard stainless-steel surface, and they started to talk to me while giving me the drugs through the IV. I screamed, "Ouch...Ouch!" The IV was not in correctly and the fluid was getting into my tissue.

Too late—they needed to proceed with the angiogram. I could hear the doctors talking and could feel the pressure in my groin. It was a strange feeling because I was aware yet drugged, so I couldn't comprehend everything that was being said. What a surreal experience.

Out of the cath lab and in recovery, I was in a room with a temporary nurse who was flown in, since all the Minnesota nurses were on strike. Feeling extreme chest pain, I couldn't move because I had to lay flat on my back to prevent bleeding in the groin. Being drugged, talking was hard, but I managed to say to the nurse on hand, "I am in pain." I repeated over, "I need more drugs. I need more drugs."

I felt extreme, dagger-sharp stabbing, and fiery pain in my chest. I realized, *I am having a heart attack, and I am going to die.* My jaw and mouth were aching and throbbing in pain. Never before in my life had I felt such jaw pain. I was sweating and nauseous. I thought, *I am dying. I am going to die in recovery. I really think I am going to die if the pain does not stop soon.*

After about an hour, I said after many attempts, "I need more drugs. I need more…I need more…"

The nurse tending to me said, "You're getting a slow drip, and that is all you're going to get."

I then said, "I need my mom. Get my mom."

I didn't know what else to do. It was clear to me this nurse was not going to listen to me and did not care. I was going to die in recovery. It was a strange and scary feeling, to feel hopeless and think, *I am going to die.*

My mom came in, and exhausted, I managed to say, "I need more meds. I am in pain. I am in pain."

My mom looked at the IV and discovered it was not working. There was something inside the IV drip that was blocking the opening, so I was not getting any pain killers. She said to the nurse, "The IV is not open. She is not getting any pain-killer medication!"

The next thing I heard: "We are moving her to ICU."

I was told I would feel more comfortable in the ICU. My body was in so much pain, sweating, and my jaw hurt. I just wanted to die.

The ICU experience was equally horrific. I begged the nurse to catheterize me since I knew I would not be able to use a bed pan while lying flat on my back. The nurse on hand said he could not give me a catheter unless my bladder registered at a full measurement. He took an ultrasound wand, and my bladder was full and met his requirement. The nausea and sweat continued for hours. I went from throwing the blanket and sheet off me to being chilled and shivering. The nurses in ICU talked all night long, left the lights on, and all I wanted to do was die.

I couldn't stand lying on my back anymore. I pled with the nurse to let me get up and take the cath out of me. It had felt like a wet diaper on me for hours, and I wondered if she had emptied it at all. It was *the* most miserable night.

At 6 a.m., I was getting up, regardless of whether they liked it or not. They had to remove the weights on my groin, then put extreme weight and pressure on me, sending me to scream, "I just want to go home!"

I wanted out of this hospital and the entire horrific twenty-four-hour experience. I had an EKG in the morning. No one told me anything. My cath doctor came to talk to me and said, "Well, we think we will let you go home today."

It was not protocol to go from the ICU to being released the next morning. It was typical procedure to go to a regular hospital room for at least one night. The nurse asked me if I had chest pains. I said I did. The pains were not as severe as they were the night before when I ended up in ICU, but they were still there.

A female cardiologist did the rounds and checked in on me a couple of hours later. I told her I was going home, that the cath doctor said it was okay. She was not okay with that decision. She said, "Based on your complication during the procedure, I don't think it is a good idea."

I asked, "What complication? I think I had a heart attack."

Her reply to me was, "Well, they did not want to do the blood test to confirm it." The look she gave me, however, told me, *Yes, you did have a heart attack.*

♥

I was supposed to rest and recover at home. I was in denial. No one knew I'd had this procedure done except immediate family. I still felt ashamed and embarrassed about my condition. I didn't allow myself to rest. I jumped right back into my company within twenty-four hours, not allowing myself to realize what my body had just gone through. I was in denial that I'd had a stent inserted and a heart attack. Four days after being released from the hospital, I went to a grocery store to do a demo, but after two hours, I felt very sick and realized that my body was not up to standing and doing a physical demo. I told myself, *I guess I better go home and lie down.*

I never posted on social media. I never wanted prayers or sympathy from strangers or acquaintances. I was a private person and kept most things to myself. I didn't really know how to process it all at fifty-one years old.

So I did what I do best—I worked. I am a workaholic and probably will be until the day I die. I decided there were two ways for me to process this disease. Number one: get involved with the American Heart Association. I could share my story to help other women and prevent them from being misdiagnosed. Number two: develop a new heart-healthy, sodium-free spice line. I was confident this could help others, and it would help me deal with the fact I had heart disease. I must admit—I love salt; I always have loved salt and over-salted my food. I knew coming out with a salt-free line would help me live a healthier lifestyle. I started working on it without telling anyone or sharing my story publicly. I decided to stop selling my caramels due to their short shelf life. Ending one product line made it the perfect time to pick up a new line that aligned with my need for healthier lifestyle choices.

♥

IN THE SPOTLIGHT

Luvafoodie®

WINTER 2017

I launched my six new salt-free Luvafoodie® spice blends in February 2017 on WCCO-TV during heart month. They included Happy Heart, an everyday salt-free spice blend; Chili Lime, a great blend to use on fish and chicken and especially good for tacos; Countryside Herb, good for vegetables and chicken; Ginger Lime, mostly ginger to use on chicken and fish; Citrus Lovers, my favorite salt-free spices to use on fish, chicken, and shrimp; and lastly, Garlic and Green Herb, to use on chicken, fish, and vegetables. I was proud to add these six blends to my existing spice blend selection.

The other spices in Luvafoodie® portfolio were Garlic Lovers, Meat Lovers, Seafood Lovers, Chicken Lovers, Smokehouse Lovers, BBQ Lovers, Sesame Lovers, Umami, and Margarita. Over the last eight years, I had launched seventeen different flavors, all of them natural with no artificial ingredients and gluten free, except for Umami, which contains soy sauce.

♥

SPRING 2017

May Day in Minnesota turned out cold, snowy, and rainy, all in the same day. Although the snow was not accumulating, it was not feeling like the first day of spring but rather the first day of March. It was depressing that the sun had not been out for days after cold, wet April. Living in Minnesota felt hard, due to the long, cold winter months. We were all ready for some natural vitamin D sunshine. The weather, I believe, signified where my heart and soul were that day. In my mind and body, depressed reigned.

Still a ray of sunshine pierced the clouds. I was meeting with the American Heart Association that day. I had an interview for the 2018 Ambassador position. Each year they select five women to tell their story and be part of their Go Red for Women campaign. I was hoping to be selected for my story of being misdiagnosed. I believed my story would inspire other women. I wanted to share it to help other women fight heart disease. It still seemed surreal to me that I had heart disease. There were many days when I couldn't process that and again, I was in denial. The interview went well. I was videotaped sharing my story.

As a result, I was one of the five women selected for the Twin Cities Go Red Ad Campaign for the next year. I would be doing various media and speaking engagements over the following twelve months. I was honored to be selected as a Brand Ambassador. From the time I found out I had heart disease, it was my goal to get involved with the American Heart Association. I knew I could deal with having heart disease if I made a difference helping other women.

First I needed to share my misdiagnosis story to help others. I'd found the reason it happened exactly as it did. It was now one of my purposes in life to advocate against heart disease. I wanted to tell the world about what happened to me. I felt empowered and excited to start this Brand Ambassador volunteer position, knowing this was the beginning of a lifelong involvement with the American Heart Association.

♥

SUMMER 2017

I turned fifty-two on July 2, kicking off what I hoped to be an exciting year ahead. I had Kathleen, my friend and psychic, over to my house a couple of weeks prior, and she told me a lot of exciting things were on the horizon.

Kathleen had always been accurate. She had predicted I would come out with cheese when cheese was the farthest thing from my mind, and she predicted my involvement with the American Heart Association and their Heart Walk.

Kathleen's reading was very positive, saying that I would get the Super Bowl contracts and it would be *big*. She said I would do five out of ten events. She said the next year, I would write two books; they would be sold as companions. In addition, I would come out with a cookbook. She saw the next years in cycles of three and five, building business. She said the next year, I would have a national TV show, something with the Food Network. Food Channel would be interested in a healthy cooking show, with me as the host and invited guests. Time would tell what the next twelve months would bring.

I had been waiting to hear back from the Super Bowl committee. I had a good feeling, based on my pitch in March of 2016, that Luvafoodie® company would be selected. I received a congratulations letter from the Business Connect program, awarding Luvafoodie® a spot in the NFL Resource Guidebook for the Super Bowl. I was thrilled and scared at the same time. I didn't find out any more details other than my company was an approved vendor. I hoped the contracts would start to come in by September. It was exciting, and it would be a life-changing event to participate in for me and my company. I expected it would take Luvafoodie® company to a national level in 2018.

When I'd turned fifty-one the year before, I had no idea I had heart disease or would end up having a heart attack. I had no idea I would launch a salt-free spice blend and cheese curds, and be approved as a Super Bowl vendor. I was realizing that life has no road map. The past year had been one of the hardest years of my life.

I embraced turning fifty-two because I was smarter, wiser, and more confident than I was a year before. I needed to stay focused for the next several months to make the Super Bowl gig a huge success. I knew I could do it, since I had come so far in just three years. I was a strong woman and had to remind myself of this when I was feeling weak. There were many days when the thought crossed my mind that I should quit and give up.

I was in a self-reflective mood. I had two big anniversaries approaching. My company, Luvafoodie, was about to turn three years old. I thought back on the last three years, and it felt more like ten years. The company and focus had changed since my original idea. It started as an online dating website for singles who were also foodies. It was now a consumable brand, consisting of spices, chocolates, and cheese curds.

Many entrepreneurs and businesses would say it was a bad idea that I never had a business plan. My approach with the company was to always work hard at it. As an entrepreneur, it was important to pivot and make changes when something was not working. If I'd had a business plan, it would have been related to an online-dating website; so by now, it would have been obsolete.

I guess you could say I am a problem solver. It was easy to know when to exit the caramel business. And it did not take me long to realize the dating component of Luvafoodie® company would never work, since I could not get critical mass or make money at it. It took me two years to transition into a consumable food company. It took two years to have enough products to make and sell at retail. Thus, as I approached year three, I looked back with a lot of pride at what I had accomplished. I applauded myself that I innovated enough products to go to market in lightspeed fashion. I also commended myself for developing a salt-free spice line and dark chocolate bar in response to living with heart disease.

My biggest accomplishment being in business for three years was knowing I would have my brand represented at Super Bowl 52 in Minneapolis, Minnesota.

I had been working on this goal for over a year, so I was very proud that it was happening. My vision for the next year when Luvafoodie® turned four was to have the brand in distribution at a national level. With the exposure that the Super Bowl would give Luvafoodie, this seemed to be a realistic goal. I predicted that within a year, there would be enough money to have some staff support with retail, so I would not be doing demos every weekend. And I hoped to secure enough business that I'd be able to hire someone to do my bookkeeping.

I looked back and a year ago, August 29, 2016, came to my mind. I wondered how I was going to feel on the anniversary of August 29, the day a year ago when I had my first angiogram due to chest pains and shortness of breath, the results of which determined I had 80 to 90 percent blockage in my ADL artery.

What if I'd known the next six months of my life were going to be a whirlwind? That I was going to meet some interesting people, via both the Super Bowl and my Brand Ambassador position for the American Heart Association?

A wise old sage would ask, "Okay, Michelle, what have you learned from this?"

My mind was still processing the answer to this question. I knew there were several lessons garnered from the past year, starting with the most important—to trust my instincts, always. I am highly intuitive and have always listened to my intuition, but due to not processing my heart disease, I blocked my intuition and looked the other way.

Lesson 1: TRUST YOUR INTUITION

This is probably the best advice I can give anyone. Always trust your intuition. The inner voice that guides us to know right from wrong is ever present. I think our mind and body work together; when one is off, the other reacts. Your body is telling you something is not right by giving you signs. In the future, I will trust all signs that my mind and body are giving me.

Lesson 2: BE STRONG

I felt weak for the first time in years and lost sight of my own strength to deal with heart disease. I learned from an early age how to process stress and survive. The coping skills I developed as a child made me good at being strong. Adverse and problematic situations force us to become strong.

Lesson 3: HAVE FAITH

Having faith helped me get through the first year of living with heart disease. I started to meditate often, and I believe it gave me the sense of peace that I needed to cope.

♥

September 19 was my one-year anniversary from having a stent put in my left anterior descending artery (LAD) and then having a heart attack in recovery. I felt happy to be alive and to have survived a difficult and challenging year.

I woke up to the news that there had been a massive shooting in Las Vegas. I don't understand evil. I don't understand the mentality of someone killing. I don't understand how to make sense of it and move on.

All day, I struggled with working, not motivated or caring.

I was moved by a podcast I listened to from one of my LinkedIn connections. It was an hour long, and I had no idea it was going to affect me the way it did. This man shared his story of a divorce and the heartache it caused his two sons. He continued to share his faith in God and how he read the Bible to help him. He then shared how his nineteen-year-old son took his own life in 2016, and he began to cry. I was touched by this stranger who no longer felt like a stranger but a strong, caring man. I was inspired by how I wanted to reach out to him and how I wanted him in my life.

I had become spiritual the past several months. Meditation helped me process what I had been through and what my purpose was. Listening to this man, I found comfort that my bigger purpose in life was to help others and trust in the direction God was leading me in.

As a result of Luvafoodie® being accepted in the NFL Resource Guidebook for the Super Bowl, the company was being considered for a VIP Super Bowl Tailgating event prior to the Super Bowl at the Minneapolis Convention Center. They were interested in the cheese curds and Belgian chocolate-covered sugar cookies. I was nervous, but at this point, I had put everything into developing the lines for the Super Bowl. The quality of my products was great, and there was no reason they should not take both lines in for the event. While I was excited for the opportunity, my heart was aching for all those who died in the Las Vegas shooting, along with their families and friends.

I worked on healing my heartbreak by being of service. I had my private NFL Super Bowl tasting with NFL contractors. The agreement was to provide them with a serving of cheese curds and cookies. The theme of the VIP event included foods representing Minnesota. Cheese curds are typically a Midwestern food. My cookies were good and made a list for the tasting. I had a mold made with the US Bank Stadium logo on it, so the chocolate which covered the shortbread cookie donned the emblem. The tasting went okay. I wouldn't know until the beginning of November if Luvafoodie® company had been selected for the VIP event. The event would host NFL owners and celebrities. It would be a once-in-a-lifetime experience for me and hopefully, give my brand and company the exposure it needed.

I meditated daily then. I'd found meditation in February 2017 after thinking I was going to die. Mediation got me through each day, and faith in God was now my driving force.

I was exhausted from every weekend doing a spice demo or a chocolate demo. Standing for a long period of time on cement floors and talking nonstop was taking its toll. I understood that with any new food item, the customer needed to taste it before they would purchase it. This was especially true for spices. It was now the fourth quarter, so I needed to be in the stores to get holiday sales.

On a positive note, I gained distribution on Amazon.com. I was doing all the individual orders for Amazon versus warehousing the line at Amazon, which worked well because I could really keep my finger on the pulse of customer interest and demand.

The bottom line—working in the stores and with the public can be humbling and exhausting. In general, most customers are nice, but there were always a few that left me speechless, with comments that can't even be repeated here.

October was defining for me. I had just launched a new spice line called the Lovers Spice Collection, to tie into the Luvafoodie® brand. Though I was not sure it was the best time to go into the fourth quarter with a new line, I did it. I was pushing myself hard because I wanted to make sure everything was perfect if I did indeed get a Super Bowl contract. I wanted the assortment to be 100 percent right and the website to be correct.

My body still ached. I was tired of working 6 a.m. to 8 p.m. every day. I was trying to stay positive and hopeful.

So much happened the following month. After going through three phases of contracts and a tasting, Luvafoodie® cookies and cheese curds were officially chosen to be one of the vendors for the VIP Super Bowl Tailgating event! We would serve plain and Bloody Mary cheese curds (that was the seasoning name, they were non-alcoholic), as well as the cookies featuring the stadium emblem. My company was featured in the NFL Business Connect newsletter. I felt honored and overwhelmed.

It was *very* exciting. I don't think it really hit me until I had to gather up my support team for the event. I had to go through a portal that required extensive FBI background checks on everyone working there. I had a close friend and a cousin run the cookie tables. I teamed with the Metz Creamery staff to run the cheese curd table. This was a private event for 10,000 people, including NFL owners and movie stars. It was not open to the public, so the screening of the thirty-five vendors selected was extensive. Luvafoodie® had made the cut!

I was featured by writer Kach Howe on *HuffPost,* in an article about my company and journey—what is honor to receive this exposure.

♥

DECEMBER 2017

Luvafoodie® expansion was starting to happen. We added distribution of the cheese curds to Festival Foods. The new Lovers Spice Collection was also going to be distributed by Coborn's Inc., for delivery and in stores at Coborn's, Ca$h Wi$e, and Festival Foods.

The countdown to the Super Bowl was on. In January, the Go Red for Women event for the American Heart Association would begin, so I would be even more busy. I was hoping to finish my book sometime after the Super Bowl. I was not sure how my journey would turn out. I knew I would be exposed to many people at this VIP event; some could even be investors.

I was also going to have my picture featured on billboards in February in the Twin Cities as part of my Brand Ambassador position. January and February proved to be the wildest, craziest months of my life. I was excited, nervous, and stressed about how I was going to juggle and manage my calendar.

I was still working every weekend doing spice demos at local grocery stores. I would come home emotionally and physically drained. I had no one at the end of the day to pump me up or fill me up. I knew I had to emotionally and physically rally until mid-February. I then needed to take a break. I couldn't afford to take a vacation, but if I didn't get away for a few days, I would not be able to keep up the pace of the past three and a half years.

I was hoping the Super Bowl event and the American Heart position would bring increased interest in my brand and company. I needed investors to come on board, and I needed to expand distribution across the USA. If I had some financial freedom, I could start to think about gaining balance in my life.

The last day of 2017, I looked back at the past twelve months with mixed emotions. I had done my last spice demo of the year the day before. It felt good to be done with demos for a while.

I would wake up on the first day of 2018 focused on continuing to succeed. The next six weeks would be the biggest career weeks of my life, with the Super Bowl event, the American Heart Association event, and the Brand Ambassador billboard going up to build awareness against heart attacks. Though I had a lot of positive things to focus on in 2018, I was not sure how my book would end. I meditated for answers. I prayed my hard work over the past three and a half years would take my brand national by the end of 2018.

♥

JANUARY 2018

The Minnesota Vikings were now in the playoff games. The "Minnesota Miracle," where Vikings player Diggs caught the football the last twelve seconds of the playoff game on January 14, 2018, was amazing. It looked like the Saints were going to win. They were ahead by a few points, with only fourteen seconds remaining. It was truly a Minnesota Miracle that everyone in the state and in the NFL was talking about. One more playoff game against the Eagles on Sunday would determine if the Minnesota Vikings would make it to the Super Bowl.

The day before, my fourteen-year-old dog, Lucy, had had a seizure. It was very scary to watch her in pain. I was leaving to go to the Taste of NFL event when she threw up and went into a seizure. I rushed her to the vet. It looked like her calcium levels were high, which could indicate cancer. I was trying to cope with this news and devastated to think of losing her. She had been my companion and little girl for fourteen years, so I was very upset. I was praying her condition did not worsen and that she had no more seizures in the weeks to come.

I was in the homestretch now with the VIP Super Bowl Tailgating Event. I went on WCCO-TV

Midmorning on January 17 to do a Super Bowl-themed cooking segment, where I debuted our new Minnesota Chocolate Bar and Game Day Chocolate boxes. We added a Game Day Tab featuring these products to our website. I hoped to get my Minnesota Chocolate Bar into hotels. I was able to sell them in some Minnesota-themed stores and a few grocery stores. I had done everything possible to promote Luvafoodie® brand and the Big Game. I had a photo shoot with some fun 1940's hair and make-up done in Viking's T-Shirts and Shorts. The purpose of the pictures were to use them on social media to support Super Bowl 52.

The countdown began to the big VIP Tailgating event. I had been writing with the idea of a book that would tell my story. I had some American Heart Association events, so I thought the book would end around the spring of 2018.

The Vikings lost to the Eagles in the playoff game. This would take some excitement out of the VIP Tailgating event, since we were all hoping the Vikings would get into the Super Bowl.

Lucy was doing…okay. There had been no more seizures, but she continued to be sick, and I was very worried about what was going on in her little body. She sensed I was a wreck, and it was obvious I was focused on her. The stress of the twelve days approaching, plus worrying about her, had gotten to me. I was at an all-time, stressed-to-the-max level, wondering, *Is this all worth it?* I was beyond exhausted from running this one-woman show and really needed help. I needed someone to come into my life and shine a big star.

♥

My dog, Lucy, had gotten worse. She had no interest in eating food at all. I had tried everything, and nothing worked. This was a sign that she most likely had cancer. Her calcium levels continued to be elevated. I could not believe this was happening to me the week of the Super Bowl. I had prayed and prayed for her to start to eat. I couldn't force food in her. I had ordered a supplement to see if that would work. I was going to look into a couple other drugs and maybe acupuncture. How much more stress could I take in my life? I prayed to God, *Let Lucy make it through Sunday.* I had no choice but to rally and go to the Super Bowl Tailgating event as a vendor. I was sick to my stomach and overwhelmed with grief. I had not felt that much heartache in my entire life.

♥

For My Aging Dog, Lucy

You are my best friend.
I love you and will always love you.
Tonight, I see you as an old dog.
I see you are tired.
I see you want me to remember—you are still a puppy
    at heart.
I see you love me unconditionally.
I see you are aging and your body aches.
I see you won't be with me forever.
I see your days and years are limited.
I see you were the best decision I ever made.
I see you love me every day.
I see you were my comfort for years when I needed you.
I see you never failed me.
I see you were my angel I prayed for.
I see you will always be in my heart.
I know I will see you one day again.
I know I will miss you every day when you are gone.
I know I will let you go when the day comes.
I know my heart will ache for you always.
I know you have been the best thing in my life.
I know I will always love you, my little girl.
I know, Lucy, you are my best friend....

WINTER 2018

It was finally here, sixteen months later—Super Bowl Sunday. The process took longer than I thought. It had started in October 2016, with my sending the Minneapolis Super Bowl office a box of chocolates and landing our first vendor meeting. Today was the day I had been working towards for months. I was glad it was here, and I would be glad when it was over.

The day started early on February 4, 2018, taking Lucy to the kennel at 7 a.m. since it would be a long one and I could not leave her alone. I was filled with anxiety about leaving her at the kennel. She was sick. What if she had a seizure? I had no choice but to take her in.

I would meet up with the owners of Metz's Heart-Land Creamery and we would do the VIP Super Bowl Tailgating Event at the Convention Center in Minneapolis, MN. The event was for 10,000 VIP people. It was an exciting but long day. The plain and Bloody Mary Cheese Curds were offered at our table. I was hoping to see some movie stars and entertainers but did not. The experience was a once-in-a-lifetime kind of day.

The day ended with my team being tired, and now I needed to pick up Lucy. My prayers were answered; she was okay, and we were both home that night together.

I prayed that she would make it through, and she did, so I was thankful.

♥

I was still fatigued from the Super Bowl and very distracted due to my dog's condition. She threw up again and then went two days without eating. It broke my heart, and I was having a very hard time focusing on my business. Several meltdowns ensued.

But first, it was time for me to put on my American Heart Brand Ambassador hat. I was going to walk in the Go Red for Women Fashion Show at the Mall of America. I would be promoting the event on My Fox Morning News on February 9. I was hoping to share my story of being misdiagnosed to help other women in the future. Getting involved with the American Heart Association was the only way I was able to process my heart attack and procedure.

It was the middle of winter, and a huge snowstorm was happening in Minnesota. I was ready for this winter to end; it had been an extremely long and difficult past few months. At the end of January, I had switched vets and took Lucy to Skadron Animal Hospital, where she was given a new diagnosis. Dr. Teri said she had a mass in her stomach but did not think she had brain cancer like the old vet had told me in December 2016. Lucy seemed ready in some ways now. She was not eating as much and sleeping most of the time. I was at a crossroads, deciding I must stop all the medication and let her go. It was a battle each day to try to get any of the meds in her. I had never felt such pain and sorrow in my life. I wanted to honor her and not force her to stay with me. I prayed for strength and courage.

♥

SPRING 2018

It was a cold day on Easter Sunday. Spring continued to be cold and drag on. This was always my favorite season, a time for new beginnings and a fresh start.

It had been a hard couple of months. Lucy had been to the ER animal hospital twice. I had her on three meds now—an appetite stimulant, an anti-nausea, and seizure medication. She'd had three seizures since the end of January. The mass in her stomach remained the same. She had gained some weight, and the medications seemed to improve her overall wellness. She seemed happy and was not in pain. I was the one suffering. I watched her and asked myself, *Am I doing the right thing?* I felt I was, but it was hard to know. I was trying not to be selfish and keep her alive because I was not ready to say goodbye. My new vet, Dr. Teri, assured me she would tell me if Lucy started to decline and lost the will to live.

I knew she had almost died the end of January. I watched her stop eating with a look of despair. She had come back to life, for how long I didn't know. It was hard to live each day, wondering and worrying about her. I didn't like to be gone for long periods of time. It took me from morning to night to feed her. It was painfully stressful, and I was not sleeping well.

My love for my dog, who seemed like my only child, had inspired me to create a new line. It was funny how life seemed to inspire me to create products to solve real-life situations.

I was in the process of working on a new line of spice blends for dogs and cats. I had found the best herbs that could help aid in nutrition for dogs and cats. I planned to debut my new Cat and Dog Lovers Natural Spice Blends in June. To enter the pet wellness category with a new line was risky, scary, and mostly exciting. I planned to attend Super Zoo, a large annual pet expo, at the end of June in Las Vegas. I wouldn't have time to exhibit this year, since the two new spice blends wouldn't be ready until the beginning of June. I was hoping to go on TV in June to launch the line. I was also hoping Lucy would still be with me at the time of the lunch. My passion about animals made it feel right for me to get into the pet category.

Prior to starting Luvafoodie, I spent a couple of years in the pet industry working as an independent rep. I was hoping my new all-natural Dog and Cat Lovers Spice Blends were a big hit. The Dog Lovers Spice Blend consisted of parsley, basil, cinnamon, ginger, and turmeric. The Cat Lovers Spice Blend consisted of parsley, dill, basil, and catnip. Dogs and cats benefit from taking these herbs just like humans, with the anti-inflammatory, cognitive, and digestive support they provide. The spice blend was designed to stimulate their appetite when mixed into their dog or cat food. The amount of spice blend to use was based on the weight of the dog or cat. The label I designed for Dog Lovers Spice Blend donned a picture of Lucy. The dog and cat spices could be purchased online and, at this point, were not in many retail stores.

♥

SUMMER 2018

A lot of things had happened since I wrote last. First and foremost, Lucy was still with me. I launched the new Dog and Cat Lovers Spice Blends at the end of June. Lucy was maintaining due to the help of the most wonderful caring veterinarian, medication, acupuncture, laser treatment, and my unconditional love and hope not to give up on her. I prayed we would have a good summer together. She'd had a disc back issue and a bladder infection, but her appetite had improved and she was happy. I was blessed each day I still had her in my life. I was thankful my prayers had been answered. I was glad the launch was over and hoped some pet specialty retailers would pick up the new line. The response had been positive overall for those who had given it to their dogs and cats. I realized it was going to take longer than I had hoped to sell it. The new line was featured in the July new products section of *Pet Age* magazine.

Luvafoodie® turned four years old on August 19. It felt like fifty years. Since the original launch date, the company had changed from an online dating website for single foodies to a consumable brand. I had expanded beyond my home state of Minnesota into a regional grocery chain in North and South Carolina.

Now Luvafoodie® was a sponsor in the August Uptown Art Festival. This was great exposure for the brand since all the chefs in the culinary challenge had to use a Luvafoodie® spice blend in their dish. It also got my spices in the Kitchen Window store.

I was at a defining moment with Luvafoodie® turning four. What was next and how long would it take to expand into other grocery retailers?

I invited Kathleen, my psychic, come to my house in the middle of July. My friend Sue was in town and wanted a reading. I ended up having one also. Kathleen picked up on my vibe, which was burnt out and tired. She also picked up on my desire to quit because I couldn't see the light at the end of the tunnel of exhaustion. I hadn't had a vacation in over four years and had put my social life and meeting someone special on hold. I was at a defining moment, again, with this company.

I needed to see what happened in the next few months and what the end of the year would look like before I decided the future of Luvafoodie. I was asking the universe to bring partners to me that would have the resources to help build the company into a national brand. I was asking the universe for the right people to come into my life to love me and grow with me.

♥

DECEMBER 2018

I was a guest on The Chris Voss Podcast show. He was an influencer rated in the top 50 by Forbes. It was a fun one-hour podcast. I felt honored by the visible attention to talk about my brand and company. I was able to chat up my new salt-free spice cookbook coming out at the end of the year and new spice gift sets.

What was the nature of this new defining moment for Luvafoodie? In 2019, I needed to raise money by getting investors to come on board. I couldn't grow the brand or make it national without funding. As scared as I was to lose control and have other people part of the scenario, it would be nice to have some financial freedom.

Christmas of 2018 was my best holiday ever, since I had my little Lucy still with me. I had always believed in miracles but more that day than ever before. It was a marvel for Lucy to still be alive and doing well overall. If you had asked me six months ago if she would still be with me at Christmas, I would have said no.

The past couple of months I had asked God to give us one more Christmas, praying for her to stay with me to finish out the year. There were some stressful days where she did not feel like eating her dog food. I took extra care to feed her more treats, to be patient with her, and to honor her feelings.

I went to church and thanked God for keeping her alive and well, for giving me an angel from heaven, which I always felt she was. I thanked the angels in heaven for hearing my prayers. We would finish this year together, and that made me feel blessed and happy.

I wanted our holiday card this year to capture the past year and how every day she was still in my life felt like a miracle. I also created a Miracle Chocolate Bar to tie into the miracle holiday card. My hope was to touch more people in the coming year with my story and give people a reason to believe and have hope.

When Lucy turned fifteen years old, we celebrated at Skadron Animal Hospital. I felt so much emotion and gratitude that I couldn't stop crying. A year ago, I never thought in a million years that we would both still be alive. She was so sick last year, and I was desperate to keep her alive through the Super Bowl. It had been a tough twelve months, no doubt, but her birthday brought a flood of gratitude and emotion. I prayed more than I had ever prayed in the past year. I prayed for her to survive, and as each period passed, I was overcome with monumental, overwhelming emotion. I thanked God that night in my mediation. I thanked Lucy for doing such a good job and staying with me.

I promised God, "If you get us to January 4, 2018, and let her turn fifteen, I will not ask any more of you." All my prayers had been answered, and I then left Lucy up to her own will to stay alive. Of course, I wanted her every day I could have her. She was not in any pain, and other than sleeping a lot and being a fussy eater, she seemed relatively good. She was on anti-seizure meds, which helped.

I always felt Lucy was an angel from Heaven. I felt it then more than ever. My future with Luvafoodie® was a big question mark, and I think she stayed with me to keep me going. We both kept going. We had a deep connection, and something told me that until there was more in place for Luvafoodie, she would not leave me.

Celebrating Lucy's birthday, I just thanked God for answering my prayers.

♥

I hired a part-time CFO (chief financial officer) to work with me on analysis and modeling projections for investor information. To expand the business, I needed funding from investors. This was a defining year; my goal was to get investors' money by June so I could hire a VP of Sales and one other salesperson. This tied into my greater goal was to be able to attend trade shows in the second half of the year. I also needed to be paid a salary.

♥

SPRING 2019

I was sitting in the cardiac intensive care unit waiting area at Fairview Hospital. My dad had a heart attack four days ago. He was having quadruple bypass surgery. I was worried and nervous. I had prayed a lot over the past few days. His blockage was 100 percent in his LAD and 80 percent blockage in the other two main arteries. Heart disease was prevalent on my dad's side of the family. All the females on his side had died of heart disease. It was no surprise my dad had heart disease. I believe he'd been having chest pains for a while but ignored them and the need to go to his doctor. When we know there is something wrong with us, fear rises and can cause denial. I had experienced the fear and denial myself.

♥

FALL 2019

I'd been very busy with demos and life. The good news was Lucy was still with me—what a trooper and bright light at the end of my days. I thanked God for all the time I was given with her and spent most of my extra time taking her to the vet for laser and acupuncture treatments. I had been syringe feeding her because she did not have many teeth and I needed to get a certain amount of food in her. She did not resist, and I gave her meds that way also. I was sure there were many people who thought I should put Lucy down. This was my decision to keep her with me. She was not suffering; she was just an aging dog. I couldn't take her life; she would decide when she was ready and when that day came, I would accept it. In the meantime, I was doing what I felt was the right thing for both of us.

I would launch my second cookbook of my grilling spices recipes in December 2019. My recipes were all easy and require very few ingredients. All the recipes could be found on my recipe tab at www.Luvafoodie. com. I tended to focus on a lot of heart-healthy recipes using vegetables, fish, and chicken. I ate very little red meat, and I didn't like to bake, so there were very few dessert recipes. My signature dish was Roasted Garlic and Herb Chicken. It reminded me of my Grandma

Rose's chicken she would make for us on Sundays. My dad's mom was a huge inspiration and part of my life while I was growing up. My grandma loved to bake and would make boxes of cookies to share with all her family at Christmas. She also was an amazing cook. My favorite dishes were her homemade ravioli with fresh ricotta cheese and her tomato sauce. I remember taking the bus with her to go to a small Italian market in St. Paul to pick up the fresh cheese. I know my grandma is looking down at me from heaven and beaming with joy. She had no idea she had such a big impact on my life and handed down to me the joy of cooking.

♥

STRANGE TIMES

Luvafoodie®

WINTER 2020

I love waking up to a new year, always my favorite day of the year. It is a fresh start, and I thought 2020 would be the year of growth for Luvafoodie. I was expanding into California with Luvafoodie® spice blends in a group of stores called Mollie Stone's Markets, an upscale family-owned grocery group out of Northern California. I was very excited, since my goal for 2020 was to go national. Another group of stores out in New York also planned to add Luvafoodie® spice blends.

My little Lucy turned sixteen years old. I was over-the-moon happy. I never thought she would still be with me. Every day was a miracle. *Thank you, God, for keeping her with me.*

For my first vacation in six years, I took my laptop with me, of course, so I could work, but it was a great vacation. My mom and I went on a Caribbean cruise. I had originally planned to organize a group of people who follow my brand Luvafoodie® to go with me. We were going to have exclusive offerings on the cruise ship for the passengers who booked under the Luvafoodie® name. It was a great idea, but the cost and timing were not right, so it ended up being just my mom and me. I had a great time, and it was nice to get away. I missed Lucy a lot, but she was in good care at the vet. I needed to have those memories with my mom, and that is what the cruise gave me.

♥

SPRING 2020

The virus Covid-19 would make history for the year 2020 across the world. We got home from our cruise in time. Only a couple of weeks later in mid-March, life halted. The virus that started in China had started to spread to the USA. Panic and fear set in, causing everyone in the world to fear this horrible virus. A lot of stores, restaurants, and bars had temporarily closed or reduced their hours. The grocery stores had to follow the state and federal rules, which meant as of the middle of March, no food demos could be in the stores. I struggled with how the life I knew and took for granted was changing and impacting my business and personal life. There seemed to be no hope and only gloom and doom. The panic caused hoarding in grocery stores. People were afraid they would run out of food and toilet paper, so they stocked up on basics and wiped out grocery stores of supplies. Masks, shields, and total fear creeped in and followed me wherever I went. I became depressed and, like everyone else in the world, scared.

It had been a long few months. I had not been able to write for a long time. I had thought about it, but the state of living in a pandemic and the fear of getting Covid-19 had paralyzed me.

Because I was unable to do demos, getting orders was tough. I had to focus on growing my online sales since many people were only shopping online for groceries. I decided to create a new line of all-natural iced teas for the spring of 2020. Instant, cold brew, all-natural iced teas was a great new category for the Luvafoodie® brand. The problem was that we were in the middle of a pandemic and no one wanted to buy anything other than essentials. The saying that timing is everything—in this case, it *really* held true. I would need to focus on online sales for the new iced teas.

SUMMER 2020

I was able to gain some local distribution of our new all-natural iced tea line. I felt hopeful since gradually parts of the state were starting to open. Life was still very different, and masks were required everywhere. I focused on the customers I had and trying to gain new ones.

♥

FALL 2020

Breaking news—Walmart.com invited me to become a vendor on their marketplace. This was a game changer! Walmart.com was the first large national retailer to get behind my brand. Other grocery and national accounts would hopefully follow in 2021. I felt this was the feather I needed in my cap after six years to feel optimistic and positive about my future.

Covid-19 had hit hard, and there were many people in the USA dying of it. My neighbor's family, a household of three, contracted the nasty disease, and it took the lives of two of them. I was saddened and depressed. I had anxiety from the fear of the upcoming months—the isolation combined with the cold weather coming.

On a positive note, my Little Lucy was still with me. She struggled but overall was doing amazing. Again I asked God to get us through the end of a year. I prayed every day that God would answer my prayers. I wanted to wake up in 2021 with Lucy, and then in 2021, she could decide her future. I wanted to finish my book. I needed to have several big things happen in 2021, so I could write a happy ending. I thought, *Luvafoodie® will take off, but still has no investors. I wonder when the day will come.* I was tired of wearing all the hats and just wanted to get through the end of 2020.

NEW YEAR'S EVE 2020

It was the last night of a horrible pandemic year full of many woes…

The year President Trump ran for second term and lost to President Elect Joe Biden.

A year unrest and violence unfolded in Minneapolis and across the country after the killing of George Floyd.

A year of toilet paper and food shortages.

A year restaurants across the country shut down and the hospitality and travel industry closed.

A year schools and colleges transitioned to online learning.

A year gyms and all indoor activities closed.

A year of fear and mistrust and anger.

A year of pain and suffering and deaths.

A year I lost two of my neighbors to Covid-19.

A year I was not able to go into any grocery stores and do demos.

A year of isolation and not seeing friends.

A year of fear.

A year I gained distribution on Walmart.com.

A year I could still celebrate being with my Little Lucy, who continued to rally and give me joy and companionship more than ever.

A year that no one would ever forget.

A year that would make history books and be remembered for changing our lives forever.

A year when no one was clear about the future.

A year some were optimistic about 2021 and others feared the horizon.

A year when the employment rate and joblessness was at an all-time high.

A year that affected all businesses, with many small cottage businesses and restaurants closing.

A year when hair and nail salons closed.

A year many feared a recession.

A year everyone was impacted by the pandemic.

♥

I was able to go sit in the garage of my manicurist, the garage door half open in April, to get my nails done, since her shop was temporarily closed. The year ended with vaccines delivered at the end of December. I hoped in my lifetime there would never be another pandemic. It felt as if nothing would ever go back to the way it was pre-pandemic.

♥

As I pondered the last night of 2020, I wondered…

What would I write next.

How long would Lucy stay with me and live?

How soon would I gain national distribution in 2021?

Would I cobrand with other brands, and if so, who would they be?

♥

I closed 2020 with high hopes for 2021, personally and professionally. I wanted to finish my book in 2021. I wanted to publish it with a happy ending. I wanted to be able to say I had a national clean-eating brand that everyone loves. Luvafoodie® *had* to take off in 2021. I was spent, and I couldn't struggle anymore. I said thank you to God for listening to and answering my most important prayers, for keeping the ones I loved with me, and for keeping me alive.

♥

MAY 28, 2021

It was the saddest day of my life. I lost my baby Lucy. She was the love of my life, best friend, and companion for seventeen and a half years. I was so sad to see her go. It went fast; she had a bad seizure on May 25. Three days later, she had constant seizures that would not stop and she stopped eating. I knew she was ready and there was nothing I could do to save her anymore. My wish was for her to turn seventeen and she did in January. She lived three and a half years longer than I expected her to live when she originally had her first seizure.

For the past three and a half years, I went to great lengths to keep her alive. She had laser and acupuncture treatments every other week. She had the best veterinary care from Skadron Animal Hospital with Dr. Teri Skadron. I helped Lucy walk and eat the past few months and did whatever I could to make her happy and comfortable.

I now had a void and hole in my heart. I didn't know what I could do to fill it or if it would ever be filled up again. So I created a line of dog spices for Lucy. I would always honor her, and she would never leave my heart. She would always be my *Heart Dog.* I knew she loved me and stayed with me as long as she could by fighting every day, especially the past six months. I told her on May 25, "It is okay to go. I love you. I know you will always be with me in spirit and in my heart."

My fear was the future. *How do I live and navigate in this house without her?* I had pictures of her all over because I wanted to remember her. She gave me so much joy and happiness over the years. She was smart and always sensed my feelings. *Did she decide to leave now because there is a lot in the works with Luvafoodie® and she needed to clear the path for me to travel and move on to whatever the future holds?* I believed she picked the date and knew I was going to accept it when she was ready. I was going to miss her day and night, especially since I worked out of my house. I was thankful for all the extra years I had with her. I was going to take the advice I gave others—one day at a time.

I didn't feel another dog coming into my life for at least a year or more. Luvafoodie® was accepted into Lomar, Hy-Vee Grocery's distribution center, for June. This gave all the stores a chance to purchase my spices. It was a big win and would open doors to other businesses who saw Hy-Vee as a competition.

I was concerned my copacker would not be able to keep up. I was having growing pains and was still a one-woman operation with no help. I didn't know what the future held for Luvafoodie, but it felt like it was going to be huge. I needed investors and funding to support the growth. I had neither, and that kept me up at night.

It was the beginning of summer, and my entire future was up in the air. I wanted to get back in shape and shed the weight I had gained due to the stress of Covid and keeping Lucy alive. The water park opened in June. I planned to go every morning for hours. I thought Lucy must have wanted me to have a summer without the stress of keeping her alive.

That was a day I would never forget; it was a defining day of loss and sadness.

💔

NEW BEGINNINGS
AND PARTNERSHIPS

Luvafoodie®

SPRING 2022

It had been one year since I said goodbye to Lucy. I had needed time to grieve Lucy and for myself. I had always felt I would have two dogs in my life, and their names were decided on years before I got both dogs. I was excited to be a new pet mom again. I wanted a breed that was different than Lucy. I love the Shih Tzu breed and grew up with a Poodle. Thus, I decided on a Shih-Poo.

It was time to pick up my new shih-poo puppy on May 28, the anniversary of Lucy's passing. Her name was Daisy, and she was my new inspiration to create a brand under Luvafoodie. I called the brand Daisy by Luvafoodie® and trademarked it as an all-natural treat. The new Daisy brand was fun, bright, and full of life, just like my dog Daisy. Her personality was a lot like Lassie as she loved everyone and every dog. She was already filling my heart up with joy, smiles, and love.

Daisy was also becoming a favorite at doggy daycare and with family and friends. We had a "Meet Daisy" celebration party a month after she came home with me. My mom threw the party at her house, and we invited friends and family to come meet Daisy. There were daisy-themed cookies, treats, and decorations. She also had a photo shoot to capture her cuteness and promote the brand.

The summer spent training and playing with Daisy was a lot of fun. My internet team, who had been with me from the beginning, designed the Daisy logo and ads. I just needed to find a pet manufacturer to create an all-natural dog treat for the Daisy brand.

WINTER 2023

I was hopeful this year my brand would expand to a national level with added distribution. I was thrilled to be featured with an article in the *Mirror Review* business magazine. Meanwhile I was waiting to find out about expanded distribution for spring 2023. I had contacted many companies on RangeMe. I sent samples and shared my distribution success stories. I needed to secure new accounts and expand distribution in order to achieve national distribution.

The year 2023 challenged me. The higher retail and inflation affected the way customers shopped. There was no loyalty to one grocery store or brand. The customer went from one retailer to the other to find the best deal. The challenging grocery store landscape impacted my business.

In the fourth quarter of the year, I had a customer request I add a small nutritional panel on the spice tin labels. The FDA did not require nutritional information on spices. Due to the cost, I decided to update only the top-selling spices with new labels. At some point, I would redo all the labels. It required me to hire a company to perform analysis on the spice blend and then have new labels printed and mailed to my copacker. This unexpected, fixed cost of goods had a negative impact on my overall profits for 2023. As a business owner, dealing with unexpected expenses was the cost of doing business. I was still a one-woman show with no investors, so cashflow was always an issue. I worked through this label issue because I had no choice in order to keep my business going.

On a positive note, I was able to add two new customers in 2023. Luvafoodie® spices were now available on Lowes.com under their grilling section. In addition, an online subscription box company, FabFitFun, picked Luvafoodie® for their fall ad-in program. Thus, the brand was growing nationally with the addition of two customers, and we made plans for more ad-in programs in 2024.

My Daisy brand was approved as a trademark this year, so now I had to focus on finding a pet company to produce an all-natural dog treat. I did not spend much time this year looking for a pet manufacturer. It would be a goal of mine in 2024.

♥

WINTER 2024

I was able to get away for a few days on a short cruise. Having not taken any time off in four years, I was in need of a break. I of course ended up making this a business trip by taking some amazing spice tin pictures and videos at different locations. I also met with the executive chef of the cruise ship. My goal was to get one of the large cruise lines to have their chefs create some Luvafoodie-inspired dishes and sell the spice blends in their gift shops.

♥

It is always important to come out with new items and keep the brand fresh. That is why I launched our new Luvafoodie® Grill Basket May 7 on WCCO-TV. Lowes.com and Amazon.com also started carrying the product. It took weeks to get a new item on their website. The cylindrical Luvafoodie® Grill Basket, perfect to use for vegetables, shrimp, and cuts of meat, comes with four Luvafoodie® spice blends. It became a huge success at the Hy-Vee stores, who sold it in their meat departments. Each rolling grill basket included one tin each of Luvafoodie's Garlic Lovers, Chicken Lovers, Seafood Lovers, and Barbeque Lovers Spice Blends. In addition, I began planning a FabFitFun promotion in August, using the grill basket for their Fall Ad-Ons.

♥

AUGUST 2024

Wow, I can hardly believe it was ten years ago that I was sweating bullets while launching the Luvafoodie® company. I remember it like it was yesterday, when I debuted an online dating website that turned into a consumable brand for foodies. It is hard to believe I built a brand from scratch and am still in business.

I look back in awe with accomplishment over the past ten years. I admire myself for sticking though each year. If you are still reading my book, you know there were many hurdles and obstacles along the way. I know the Luvafoodie® brand is here to stay. I will be celebrating ten years by doing another WCCO-TV show on August 13, celebrating our birthday.

Ten years later, my goal for the brand and company is still the same—to take the brand national in brick-and-mortar superstores across the country. I hope sharing my journey through this book helps me to accomplish this goal. I will continue to focus on local TV with the idea that one day I will be on national TV. I also hope to cobrand with other clean-eating and drinking brands in the future. I end the book feeling proud of myself with a huge sense of accomplishment.

My words and thoughts are to be continued. My story is not over yet!

As always… *Eat Clean, Drink Clean, Be Well and Stay Well.*

♥

A SPECIAL THANK YOU

I want to thank a few companies that have kept my business going.

WCCO-TV, the talented Minneapolis news station, has been supportive and inviting over the past ten years, letting me come on their midmorning show to do Luvafoodie® cooking segments.

Employee-owned **Hy-Vee Grocery Company**, which came into the Minnesota marketplace at the time I launched my spice blends. I have grown my business with them over the years and am now in their distribution center. Many of their stores use Luvafoodie® spice blends in bulk to season fish, shrimp, chicken, and meat.

Mollie Stone's Markets in Northern California. Their upscale grocery stores carry Luvafoodie® spice blends in their meat and seafood departments.

Lowes Home Improvement Company. Their online store, Lowes.com, added Luvafoodie® spices in 2023.

Skadron Animal Hospital in West Saint Paul, Minnesota. Dr. Teri and their staff kept Lucy with me for three extra years. Their patience, love, and understanding will forever stay with me.

Lastly, I would like to thank my Mom. She has supported my journey in creating Luvafoodie® brand by believing in me. She has always been my best friend and without her continued love and support I would not be the woman I am today. I love you, Mom.

♥

Luvafoodie®

RECIPES

*Use Luvafoodie® spice blends and dressing
mixes to make these delicious recipes.*

LUVAFOODIE®
CITRUS LOVERS SALAD

Delicious light salad to serve with any main dish.

Serves 6

For Luvafoodie® Citrus Lovers Salad Dressing:

½ cup olive oil
juice of 1 orange
1 tablespoon lime juice
2 tablespoons honey
2 tablespoons white balsamic vinegar
1 tablespoon **Luvafoodie® Citrus Lovers Salad Dressing & Dip Mix**

For Salad:

1 navel orange
2 Cara Cara oranges
1 grapefruit
1 endive head, sliced first lengthwise, then crosswise, in ½-inch slices
3 cups mixed greens (baby spinach, arugula, and chard)

1 cup crumbled goat cheese

1 cup candied walnuts

Directions:

1. Prepare salad dressing according to package and set aside.
2. Peel and pith (remove white inner layer) citrus fruit and thinly slice.
3. Toss all salad ingredients together in a large bowl.
4. Drizzle **Luvafoodie® Citrus Lovers Salad Dressing** on top of salad and toss.

LUVAFOODIE® HERB LOVERS WINTER SALAD

Delicious winter and holiday salad.

Serves 6

For Luvafoodie® Herb Lovers Salad Dressing:

¾ cup olive oil
¼ cup balsamic vinegar
2 tablespoons apple cider
1 tablespoon honey
1 tablespoon **Luvafoodie® Herb Lovers Salad Dressing & Dip Mix**

For Salad:

2 blood oranges
1 navel orange
1 grapefruit
1 radicchio head, cored, and roughly chopped
1 endive head, sliced, first lengthwise, then crosswise, in ½ inch slices
4 cups mixed greens (baby spinach, arugula, and chard)

½ cup pomegranate seeds

¼ cup parmesan cheese, shaved

Directions:

1. Prepare salad dressing according to package and set aside.
2. Peel and pith (remove white inner layer) citrus fruit and thinly slice.
3. Toss all salad ingredients together in a large bowl.
4. Drizzle **Luvafoodie® Herb Lovers Salad Dressing** on top of salad.

LUVAFOODIE®
HONEY MUSTARD FARRO
AND SQUASH SALAD

Colorful and tasty winter salad that
works great as a main dish.

Serves 6

For Salad:

3 cups butternut squash, peeled and cut into ½
cubes

2 cups brussels sprouts, quartered

3 tablespoons olive oil

2 tablespoons **Luvafoodie® Garlic Lovers Spice
Blend**

¾ cup farro, cooked to package instructions

4 cups romaine lettuce, chopped

½ cup dried cranberries

½ cup pecans, chopped

For Luvafoodie® Honey Mustard Salad Dressing:

1 tablespoon **Luvafoodie® Honey Mustard Lovers
Salad Dressing & Dip Mix**

½ cup olive oil

3 tablespoons apple cider vinegar
1 tablespoon lemon juice
2 tablespoons honey

Directions:

1. Preheat oven to 425°F.
2. Peel and dice butternut squash into ½-inch cubes and place on cookie sheet.
3. Drizzle with 1½ tablespoons olive oil and 1 tablespoon **Luvafoodie® Garlic Lovers Spice Blend**. Roast in oven for 30 minutes.
4. Quarter brussels sprouts. Place in bowl, drizzle with 1½ tablespoons olive oil, and season with 1 tablespoon **Luvafoodie® Garlic Lovers Spice Blend**. Add brussels sprouts to oven and roast with squash for another 20 minutes. Cool and set aside roasted squash and brussels sprouts.
5. Cook faro until tender, according to package directions. Rinse with cold water and set aside.
6. Prepare **Luvafoodie® Honey Mustard Salad Dressing & Dip Mix**.
7. On a large platter or in a large bowl, place romaine lettuce and add roasted squash, brussels sprouts, farro, cranberries, and pecans.
8. Drizzle **Luvafoodie® Honey Mustard Salad Dressing** over salad.

LUVAFOODIE®
GARLIC LOVERS
OLIVE CHEESE BREAD

This is a crowd-pleasing appetizer!

Serves 6

Ingredients:

- 1 8-ounce jar/can black olives
- 1 8-ounce jar/can green olives
- 1 cup chopped green onions
- 1 stick softened unsalted butter
- 1 cup mayonnaise
- 2 teaspoons creamy horseradish sauce
- 2 tablespoons **Luvafoodie® Garlic Lovers Spice Blend**
- 8 ounces Monterey Jack cheese
- 1 loaf French bread, sliced in half

Directions:

1. Preheat oven to 350°F.
2. Chop olives and green onions and set aside.

3. In a large bowl, mix butter, mayonnaise, horse-radish sauce, and **Luvafoodie® Garlic Lovers Spice Blend** until blended.
4. Add cheese, olives, and green onions to bowl and mix into butter mixture.
5. Spread cheese mixture evenly on cut side of French bread.
6. Put French bread, cheese spread side up, on baking sheet.
7. Bake until cheese is melted and bread is toasted, about 10 minutes.

LUVAFOODIE®
MULLED CIDER SOUP

*A flavorful starter soup to serve with
Smokehouse Lovers Cheese Puffs.*

Serves 4

Ingredients:

2 tablespoons unsalted butter

2 medium onions, thinly sliced

2 medium Honeycrisp apples, diced

6 cups chicken broth

½ cup mulled apple cider (follow **Luvafoodie® Mulling Spice Mix** package directions to make cider using 1 quart apple cider)

1 medium potato, diced

1 bay leaf

1½ teaspoons salt

1 teaspoon pepper

1 tablespoon **Luvafoodie® Garlic Lovers Spice Blend**

½ cup heavy cream

1 tablespoon lemon juice

Directions:

1. Melt butter in large Dutch pan over low heat.
2. Add onions, apples, chicken broth, mulled cider, potato, bay leaf, salt, pepper, and **Luvafoodie® Garlic Lovers Spice Blend**.
3. Increase heat to medium and cook for 35 minutes, stirring often.
4. Remove from heat, remove bay leaf, and process mixture with handheld blender until smooth.
5. Stir in cream and lemon juice. Serve with Smokehouse Lovers Cheese Puffs.

LUVAFOODIE®
SMOKEHOUSE LOVERS
CHEESE PUFFS

Serves 4

Ingredients:

1 frozen puff pastry sheet

1 large egg

2 teaspoons milk

1 tablespoon **Luvafoodie® Smokehouse Lovers Spice Blend**

½ cup grated parmesan cheese

2 tablespoons grated sharp cheddar.

½ teaspoon minced chives

Directions:

1. Preheat oven to 400°F.
2. Let puff pastry come to room temperature for 30 minutes, partially thawed.
3. Unfold pastry sheet onto lightly floured surface.
4. Whisk together egg and milk.

5. Brush pasty sheet with egg mixture and sprinkle with cheese, chives, and **Luvafoodie®️ Smokehouse Lovers Spice Blend**.
6. Cut in half to create two rectangle shapes and place them 1 inch apart on parchment paper. Bake for 10 to 15 minutes until golden brown.
7. Remove from oven and let rest a few minutes. Cut in rectangles to serve.

LUVAFOODIE® CITRUS LOVERS ASPARAGUS

Use a grilling basket to make this delicious, salt-free, heart-healthy side dish.

Serves 8

Ingredients:

1 tablespoon **Luvafoodie® Citrus Lovers Salad Dressing & Dip Mix**

½ cup olive oil

juice of one orange

1 tablespoon lime juice

2 tablespoons honey

2 tablespoons white balsamic vinegar

1 lb. asparagus

Directions:

1. Mix together **Luvafoodie® Citrus Lovers Salad Dressing & Dip Mix**, olive oil, orange and lime juices, honey, and white balsamic vinegar. Set dressing aside.

2. Rinse asparagus and cut off the end of stalks.

3. Put asparagus in grilling basket and grill for 10 minutes over medium heat
4. (or roast in 380°F oven on baking sheet for 10 minutes).
5. Plate asparagus and drizzle with **Luvafoodie® Citrus Lovers Salad Dressing**.

LUVAFOODIE®
GARLIC AND GREEN HERB
TWICE-BAKED POTATOES

Delicious low-fat and low-sodium side dish for two.

Serves 2

Ingredients:

2 medium-sized baking potatoes

1 cup of nonfat plain Greek yogurt

2 tablespoons skim milk

1 cup of low-fat mozzarella, shredded

1 tablespoon **Luvafoodie® Garlic and Green Salt-Free Spice Blend**

Directions:

Preheat oven to 400°F.

Bake potatoes for 1 hour.

Slice potatoes in half lengthwise, scoop out potato, and save potato skins.

In a bowl, mix together yogurt, milk, cheese, and **Luvafoodie® Garlic and Green Salt-Free Spice Blend**. Stir in hot potato.

Spoon potato mixture back into potato skins.
Bake for another 15 minutes.
Sprinkle with additional **Luvafoodie® Garlic and Green Salt-Free Spice Blend**.

LUVAFOODIE®
BBQ LOVERS ORANGE
CHICKEN WINGS

Great summertime BBQ sauce to use on chicken wings.

Makes 2 cups of sauce

For Luvafoodie® Orange BBQ Sauce:

½ cup minced yellow onion

1 tablespoon olive oil

1 tablespoon **Luvafoodie® Garlic Lovers Spice Blend**

2 cups ketchup

⅓ cup apple cider vinegar

½ cup brown sugar

½ cup honey whiskey

⅓ cup Worcestershire sauce

½ cup orange juice

3 tablespoons of **Luvafoodie® Barbeque Lovers Spice Blend**

For Wings:

1 dozen chicken wings
Luvafoodie® Orange BBQ Sauce
1 tablespoon orange zest

Directions:

1. Preheat oven to 375°F or grill at medium heat.
2. In a saucepan, sauté onions with olive oil and **Luvafoodie® Garlic Lovers Spice Blend**.
3. Add ketchup, apple cider vinegar, brown sugar, whiskey, Worcestershire sauce, orange juice and **Luvafoodie® Barbeque Lovers Spice Blend to saucepan**.
4. Simmer BBQ sauce for 20 minutes and set aside.
5. Put wings in ovenproof pan (or on the grill) and brush with **Luvafoodie® Orange BBQ Sauce**.
6. Bake in oven for 35 minutes or grill covered for 30 minutes. Top with more BBQ sauce and orange zest.

LUVAFOODIE®
SUMMER BBQ CHICKEN

Delicious dinner bursting with BBQ chicken flavor.

Serves 6–8

For Luvafoodie® Smokehouse Lovers BBQ Sauce:

½ cup minced yellow onion

1 tablespoon olive oil

1 tablespoon **Luvafoodie® Garlic Lovers Spice Blend**

2 cups ketchup

⅓ cup apple cider vinegar

½ cup brown sugar

½ cup Jack Daniel's Tennessee Honey Whiskey

⅓ cup Worcestershire sauce

2 tablespoons **Luvafoodie® Smokehouse Lovers Spice Blend**

1 tablespoon **Luvafoodie® Barbeque Lovers Spice Blend**

For BBQ Chicken:

4 skinless chicken breasts

4 chicken thighs
1 tablespoon **Luvafoodie® Smokehouse Lovers Spice Blend**
1 tablespoon **Luvafoodie® Barbeque Lovers Spice Blend**
Luvafoodie® Smokehouse Lovers BBQ Sauce

Directions:

1. Preheat oven to 375°F. (Chicken can also be cooked on the grill on medium heat.)
2. In a saucepan, sauté onions with olive oil and **Luvafoodie® Garlic Lovers Spice Blend**.
3. Add ketchup, apple cider vinegar, brown sugar, whiskey, Worcestershire sauce, **Luvafoodie® Smokehouse Lovers Spice Blend** and **Luvafoodie® Barbeque Lovers Spice Blend to saucepan**.
4. Simmer **Luvafoodie® Smokehouse Lovers BBQ Sauce** for 20 minutes.
5. Put chicken breasts and thighs in ovenproof pan. Sprinkle with **Luvafoodie® Smokehouse Lovers Spice Blend** and **Luvafoodie® Barbeque Lovers Spice Blend**.
6. Bake for 35 minutes. Top with **Luvafoodie® Smokehouse Lovers BBQ Sauce** and bake for another 5 minutes. (For another option, cook chicken on the grill and top with BBQ sauce 5 minutes before done.)

LUVAFOODIE® MARGARITA SHRIMP TACOS WITH CILANTRO LIME SLAW

Makes 10 street tacos

For Tacos:

> 2 tablespoons lemonade
> 3 tablespoons olive oil
> 2 tablespoons **Luvafoodie® Margarita Spice Blend**
> 1 pound thawed shrimp, deveined (or use chicken or fish)
> 10 street taco tortillas

Coleslaw ingredients:

> 3 cups shredded green cabbage (core removed)
> 1 bunch cilantro, chopped
> 2 jalapeños, finely chopped
> 2 tablespoons lime juice
> 1 tablespoon **Luvafoodie® Margarita Spice Blend**
> 3 tablespoons olive oil

Directions:

1. In a frying pan, add lemonade, olive oil, **Luvafoodie® Margarita Spice Blend**, and shrimp.
2. Sauté until shrimp is opaque, for about 10 minutes, and set aside.
3. In a bowl, combine all ingredients for coleslaw and set aside.
4. Warm tortillas in oven or microwave.
5. Top tortillas with shrimp and then coleslaw.

LUVAFOODIE®
SEAFOOD LOVERS
SHRIMP LETTUCE WRAPS

*Healthy, easy, delicious summer entrée
to serve for lunch or dinner.*

Serves 4

For Wraps:

    1 pound thawed shrimp, deveined
    1 tablespoon olive oil
    1 tablespoon **Luvafoodie® Seafood Lovers Spice
    Blend**
    1 head Bibb lettuce
    Pineapple Salsa

For Pineapple Salsa:

    1 cup diced pineapple
    1 cup diced tomatoes (red, yellow, and orange)
    ½ cup chopped cilantro
    ½ cup red pepper diced
    1 tablespoon lime juice
    ¼ cup diced red onion
    2 tablespoons diced jalapeño
    1 teaspoon **Luvafoodie® Garlic Lovers Spice Blend**

Directions:

1. Preheat grill to medium. (Shrimp can also be cooked in a frying pan.)
2. In a bowl, mix together shrimp, olive oil, and **Luvafoodie® Seafood Lovers Spice Blend**.
3. Add shrimp to grilling basket and place on grill. Turn grill basket with wire tool that comes with grill basket. Cook or grill shrimp until opaque, about 10 minutes.
4. In a small bowl, combine pineapple, tomatoes, cilantro, red pepper, lime juice, onion, jalapeño, and **Luvafoodie® Garlic Lovers Spice Blend to make pineapple salsa**.
5. Separate Bibb lettuce into individual leaves.
6. Top each piece of lettuce with 3–4 grilled shrimp and pineapple salsa.

LUVAFOODIE® SALMON IN CAPERS MARINADE

Healthy, tasty salmon recipe for two.

Serves 2

For Capers Marinade:

2 tablespoons extra virgin olive oil
2 tablespoons white wine
2 tablespoons lemon juice
2 tablespoons capers
1½ teaspoons **Luvafoodie® Garlic Lovers Spice Blend**

For Salmon Filets:

2 8 oz. filets of salmon, skin removed
capers marinade
microgreens, for garnish

Directions:

1. Preheat oven 375°F.
2. In a baking dish, combine olive oil, wine, lemon juice, capers, and **Luvafoodie® Garlic Lovers Spice Blend**.
3. Roll each filet in marinade.
4. Bake for 20 minutes.
5. Plate baked salmon on two plates and top with micro greens. Serve with roasted potatoes or your favorite vegetable and Luvafoodie® Winter Salad.

LUVAFOODIE®
MEAT LOVERS BITES

Delicious appetizer for game days.

Serves 4

For Tenderloin Bites:

1 pound cubed tenderloin

2 tablespoons olive oil

2 teaspoons **Luvafoodie® Meat Lovers Spice Blend**

For Horseradish Sauce:

¾ cup sour cream

1 tablespoon creamy horseradish sauce

1 teaspoon **Luvafoodie® Meat Lovers Spice Blend**

2 tablespoons chopped green onions

Directions:

1. In a frying pan, sauté tenderloin with olive oil and 2 teaspoons **Luvafoodie® Meat Lovers Spice Blend** until medium cooked.
2. In a bowl, combine sour cream, creamy horse-radish sauce, and 1 teaspoon **Luvafoodie® Meat Lovers Spice Blend**.
3. Top sauce with chopped green onions. Serve with cooked tenderloin bites.

LUVAFOODIE® SMOKEHOUSE PORK TENDERLOIN WITH BLUEBERRY RHUBARB SAUCE

Delicious, tasty dinner bursting with flavor.

Serves 4

For Tenderloin:

1 pork tenderloin
1 tablespoon olive oil
1 tablespoon **Luvafoodie® Smokehouse Lovers Spice Blend**

For Potatoes:

12 small yellow potatoes
1 tablespoon olive oil
1 tablespoon **Luvafoodie® Garlic Lovers Spice Blend**

For Blueberry Rhubarb Sauce:

½ cup Mrs. Fromley's Blueberry Rhubarb Dessert Jam
½ cup Trader Joe's Raspberry Vinegar
½ teaspoon **Luvafoodie® Garlic Lovers Spice Blend**

For Garnish:

1 package fresh rosemary
½ cup fresh blueberries

Directions:

1. Preheat oven to 350°F.
2. Rub pork tenderloin with olive oil and **Luvafoodie® Smokehouse Lovers Spice Blend.**
3. Put on baking sheet in oven for 30 minutes.
4. Coat potatoes with olive oil and **Luvafoodie® Garlic Lovers Spice Blend.** Wrap potatoes together in foil and put in oven for 30 minutes.
5. In a small saucepan, combine jam, raspberry vinegar, and **Luvafoodie® Garlic Lovers Spice Blend** and cook on low heat for five minutes, then set aside.
6. Remove pork tenderloin from oven and let rest for 5 minutes before slicing in ½" pieces.
7. On a serving plate, arrange sliced pork tenderloin and potatoes. Top pork tenderloin with blueberry rhubarb sauce. Garnish with rosemary sprigs and blueberries.

LUVAFOODIE®
MULLED CIDER
MINI-BUNDT CAKES

You can serve this delicious fall dessert with vanilla ice cream.

Makes 12 mini cakes

For Cakes:

1 box yellow cake mix

¾ cup mulled apple cider (follow **Luvafoodie®**
Mulling Spice Mix package directions to make)

½ cup unsweetened applesauce

3 large eggs

2 tablespoons unsalted butter, melted

1 tablespoon brown sugar

1 teaspoon vanilla

For Glaze:

¼ cup butter

¼ cup water

1 cup sugar

½ cup apple liqueur

Directions:

1. Preheat oven to 350°F.
2. In a large mixing bowl, use handheld mixer and combine cake mix, apple cider, applesauce, eggs, and melted butter.
3. Add brown sugar and vanilla, mixing well.
4. Grease and flour 12 mini-Bundt pans. Pour batter into pans.
5. Bake for 40 to 50 minutes or until a toothpick comes out clean.
6. After 15 minutes, turn the Bundt pans over onto a cooling rack.
7. In a medium saucepan, melt butter.
8. Stir in water and sugar. Boil for 5 minutes, stirring constantly.
9. Remove from heat. Stir in apple liquor.
10. Drizzle glaze over cakes.

LUVAFOODIE®
GINGER LIME
LEMON RICOTTA KUGEL

Serves 6

Ingredients:

1 12-ounce package wide egg noodles
4 tablespoons unsalted butter, melted
1 16-ounce container sour cream, preferably full fat
1 15-ounce container ricotta, preferably whole milk or part skim
¾ cup sugar
3 large eggs, lightly beaten
zest and juice from 2 Meyer or regular lemons (about ¼ cup juice)
1½ teaspoons vanilla extract
1 tablespoon **Luvafoodie® Ginger Lime Spice Blend**
¼ teaspoon salt
½ cup dried tart cherries
½ cup golden raisins
cinnamon, for sprinkling on top as garnish

Directions:

1. Preheat oven to 375°F. Butter a 9x13-inch glass or ceramic baking dish and set aside.
2. Bring a large pot of water to a boil.
3. Add egg noodles and boil for 5 to 6 minutes.
4. Drain noodles, return them to the pot or a large bowl, and toss with melted butter.
5. In another large bowl, whisk together sour cream, ricotta, sugar, eggs, lemon zest and juice, vanilla, salt and **Luvafoodie® Ginger Lime Spice Blend.**
6. Stir in noodles, then fold in dried cherries and raisins.
7. Pour the noodle mixture into the prepared pan and smooth the top with a spatula.
8. Sprinkle top of kugel with cinnamon.
9. Bake for 45 to 55 minutes, or until the custard is set and the top is lightly browned.
10. Remove kugel from oven and allow to rest for 10 to 15 minutes before cutting.

*Tips: Leftover kugel may be stored, well covered, in the refrigerator for 2 to 3 days. Bring the kugel to room temperature or better yet, warm in the oven before serving.

LUVAFOODIE® DOG LOVERS FROZEN TREATS

Your dog will love this healthy frozen treat that packs a boost of nutrition.

Makes 12 treats

Ingredients:

3 cups plain Lifeway Kefir

½ cup organic creamy unsweetened peanut butter (no sugar or salt)

½ cup organic unsweetened plain shredded coconut

1 tablespoon **Luvafoodie® Dog Lovers Natural Spice Blend**

Directions:

1. Blend all ingredients in blender until smooth.
2. Pour into ice cube trays and freeze.

Available at:

Luvafoodie.com
Shopify
Amazon
Lowes.com

ABOUT THE AUTHOR

MICHELLE MAZZARA is an enthusiastic entrepreneur and the creator of Luvafoodie® brand and company, founded in 2014. Michelle's passion for food and beverage led her to create the brand. She followed her heart to start the first online dating website for singles who were also foodies. Food connects people, and that was the foundation of the Luvafoodie® company. After a year, Luvafoodie® morphed into creating clean food and drink products. Luvafoodie® is now a consumable brand that is found in grocery stores and online. It is a favorite clean-eating brand that consists of gourmet natural spice blends, all-natural instant cold brew iced teas, pet spices for dogs and cats, and all-natural salad dressing and dip mixes.

Luvafoodie® company is certified as MNUCP and Certified Women's Business Enterprise.

Visit Luvafoodie.com.

certified
WBENC
WOMEN'S BUSINESS ENTERPRISE

PUBLISHER'S NOTE

Thank you for your readership and the opportunity to serve you. If you would like to share this book, here are some ways:

REVIEWS:	Write an online book review
GIVING:	Gift this book to friends, family, and colleagues
BOOK CLUBS:	Read it with a group of colleagues or friends
EVENTS:	Invite the author to be speaker for your organization. Email: info@citrinepublishing.com
BULK ORDERS:	Email: sales@citrinepublishing.com
CONTACT:	Call +1-828-585-7030 or email: info@citrinepublishing.com

We appreciate your book reviews, letters, and shares.

CITRINE
PUBLISHING